Read and See

Read and See

Bill Kontzias

I Like to Read®

HOLIDAY HOUSE • NEW YORK

For Helen, Olga, and John

The publisher and photographer would like to thank Stephen Toth and Sam Toth for reviewing this book.

I LIKE TO READ is a registered trademark of Holiday House Publishing, Inc.
Text copyright © 2018 and photographs copyright © 2014 by Bill Kontzias
All Rights Reserved
HOLIDAY HOUSE is registered in the U.S. Patent and Trademark Office.
Printed and bound in October 2017 at Tien Wah Press, Johor Bahru, Johor, Malaysia.
The artwork was created in camera, tabletop photography with simple lighting schemes, designed to tell stories with minimum computer manipulation.
The photographs were taken with a high-quality digital camera and two vintage film lenses that were modified and adapted to fit current technology.
www.holidayhouse.com
3 5 7 9 10 8 6 4 2

The Library of Congress has cataloged the prior edition as follows.
Kontzias, Bill.
Look and see : a what's-not-the-same game / by Bill Kontzias. — First edition.
pages cm
ISBN 978-0-8234-2860-1 (hardcover)
1. Picture puzzles—Juvenile literature. I. Title.
GV1507.P47K68 2014
793.73—dc23
2013019678

ISBN 978-0-8234-3983-6
(ILTR paperback)

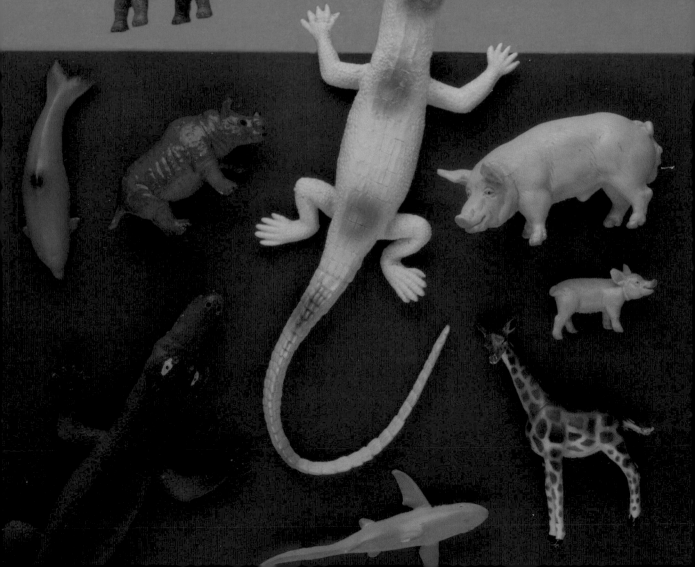

I Like to Read® books, created by award-winning
picture book artists as well as talented newcomers,
instill confidence and the joy of reading in new readers.

We want to hear every new reader say, "I like to read!"

Visit our website for flash cards, activities, and more about the series:
www.holidayhouse.com/ILiketoRead
#ILTR
This book has been tested by an educational expert
and determined to be a guided reading level E.

Read and See from the Sea

Look for

1 ball and

2 sea stars.

Dinosaur
Read and See

Look for

3 balls.

Read and See
Craft Scraps

Look for

5 sticks.

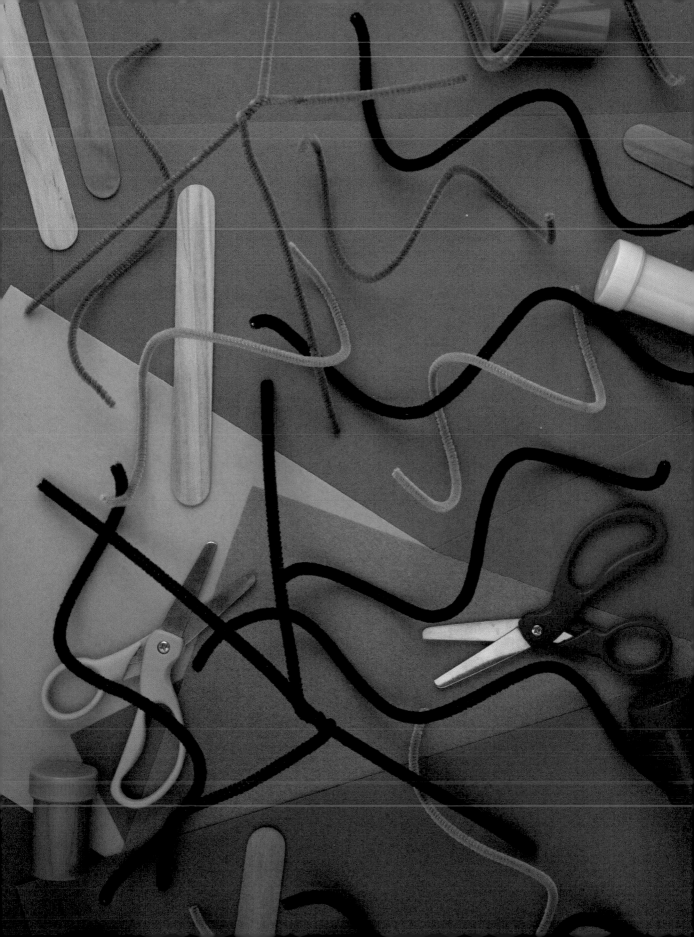

Yikes! Stripes!
Read and See

Look for

2 zebras and

1 tiger.

Read and See
Mess of Letters

Look for

4 turtles,

3 cars, and

1 snake.

Read and See
Birds and Blocks

Look for

5 balls and

1 duck.

Happy Face
Read and See

Look for

1 hat and

1 blue eye.

Tadpole-to-Frog
Read and See

Look for

2 newts.

We ♥ Buttons
Read and See

Look for

3 people and

1 newt.

Read and See
on the Road

Look for

2 pigs and

4 birds.

Float and Fly
Read and See

Look for

5 dice and

2 planes.

Read and See
Great Shapes

Look for

1 heart.

Pick-a-Color
Read and See

Look for

1 tiger and

2 birds.

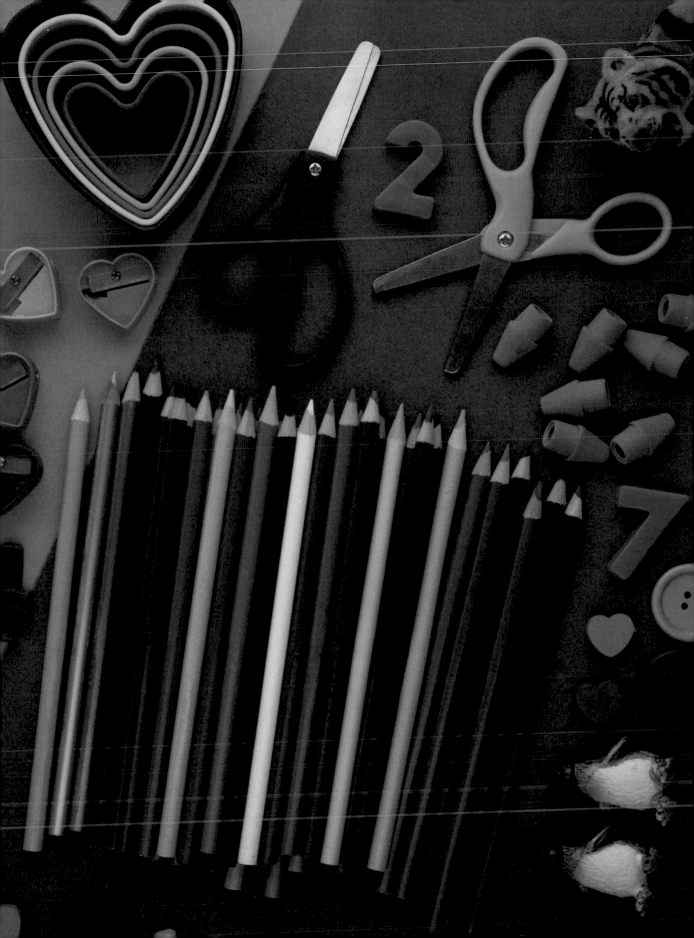

ACKNOWLEDGMENTS

I would like to give special thanks to Grace Maccarone, for her encouragement and graceful critique; Betsy and Ted Lewin, for their true friendship, for their inspiration, and for mentoring this project; Kimberley McAdoo, New York City special education teacher, for sharing her insights and expertise; and Francesco Scavullo, my once-upon-a-time photography mentor, who remarked, "My dear William, visual problems are best solved visually. Your eyes are meant for seeing!"
—B. K.